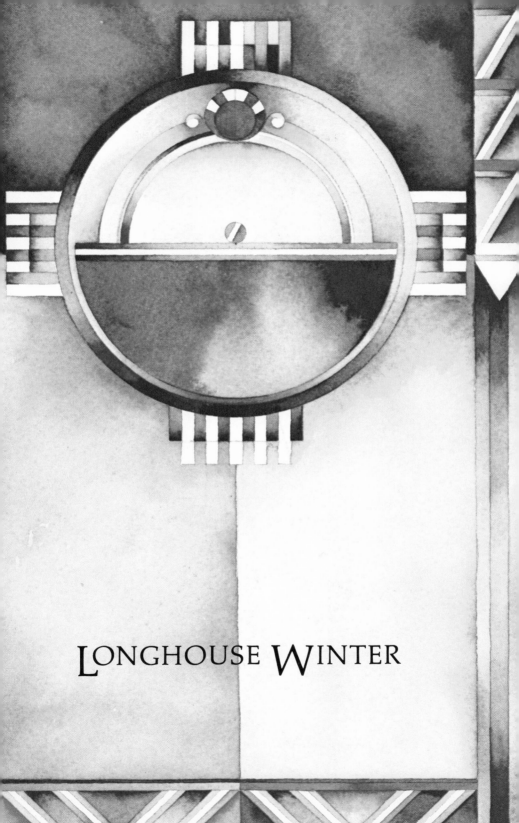

LONGHOUSE WINTER

IROQUOIS TRANSFORMATION TALES

LONGHOUSE WINTER

Adapted by Hettie Jones
Illustrated by Nicholas Gaetano

HOLT RINEHART AND WINSTON / NEW YORK   CHICAGO   SAN FRANCISCO

for Kellie and for Lisa
Hettie Jones

joy to you and me and all that's we
Nicholas Gaetano

FOREWORD

The five-nation League of the Iroquois Indians, sometimes called The Longhouse, never told the tales of their people in the summer. It was feared that a passing animal, entranced by some legend, might not find his winter home when the snow fell; or that the vine over the lodge door, listening so eagerly, would forget to let down its sap before the frost; or that the bird in his wonder and bewilderment would be unable to recall the sun way to the south, and would die in the icy blast of the north wind.

Stories were not to be told even in secret. One could never tell when a bird or bug might be listening and report the offense to the Little People, the fairy guardians of summer silence. They would not hesitate to enforce the law—by sending a bee to sting the offender's tongue!

Knowing all these things, the Iroquois kept to their farming and building in summer and saved their legends for wintertime around the longhouse fire. Only then, with the hard work done, might the magic word be said: "Hanio"—let's have a story.

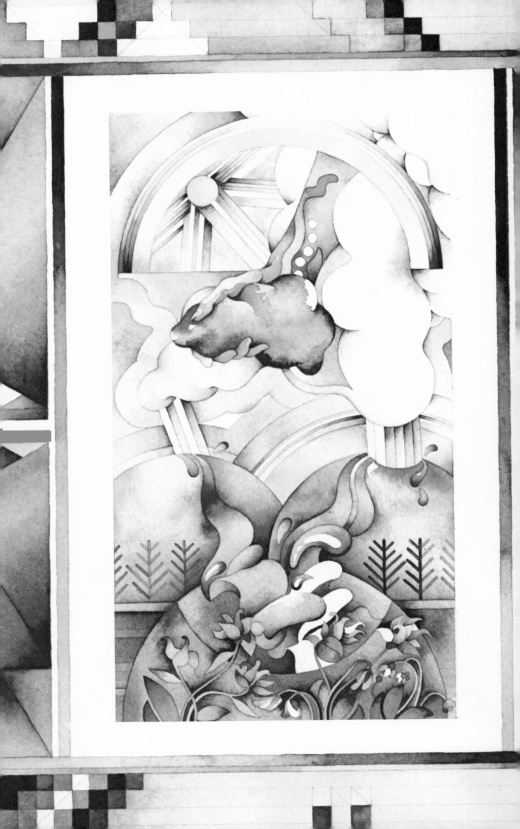

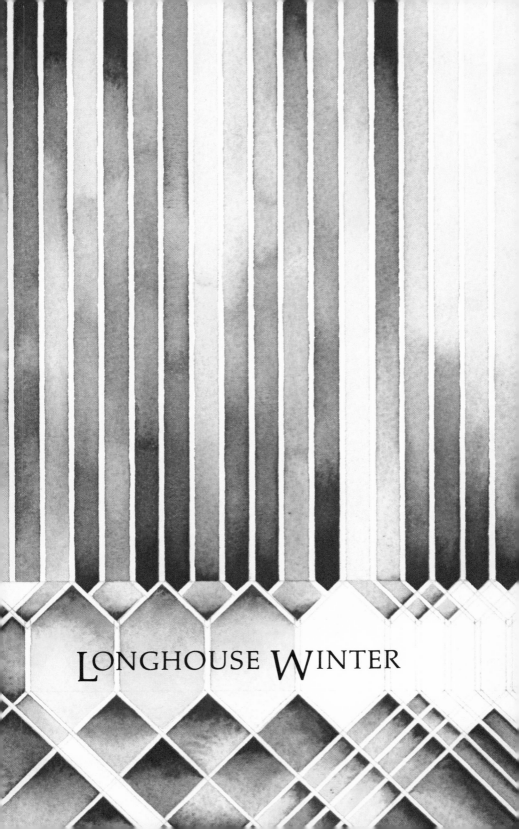

LONGHOUSE WINTER

O–go–ne–sas belonged to the Wolf clan. He was a chief's son and had been trained for the chase and the trails of the warpath. He ran the swiftest race and led in the games; he could shoot an arrow farther than any of his friends and hurl the snow snake beyond the bounds. He understood the forests and streams, and the wild game trusted him. Birds would flock at his call.

He could wander late in the forest without fear, for the bear and the wolf were as welcome to meet as the friends in his father's lodge. They knew him and would pass silently by. O–go–ne–sas was the pride of the village and the boast of his father. Everyone believed he would become a great chief.

Now the time for his Dream Fast had come. It was a time of deep snow and there were keen winds, but O–go–ne–sas was young and his blood like fire. He feared neither hunger nor cold. This was the hour of his manhood, and he welcomed its coming.

In the heart of the woods, O–go–ne–sas built a lodge of young saplings and covered it with hemlock branches for shelter from the snows. He took off his furs and prayed to the spirit of the Wolf clan to appear to him. Then he entered the lodge. Ten suns would pass above him while he waited. His Dream Fast had begun.

Alone with his thoughts, O–go–ne–sas remembered his childhood. He had been happy; no sorrow had come to him. His mother had cared for him most of the time, except when he had gone with his father to learn the ways of the forest. It was his father who had told him about the Dream Fast—how in a dream his clan spirit would bring to him a totem, a sign to be the guardian of his future life.

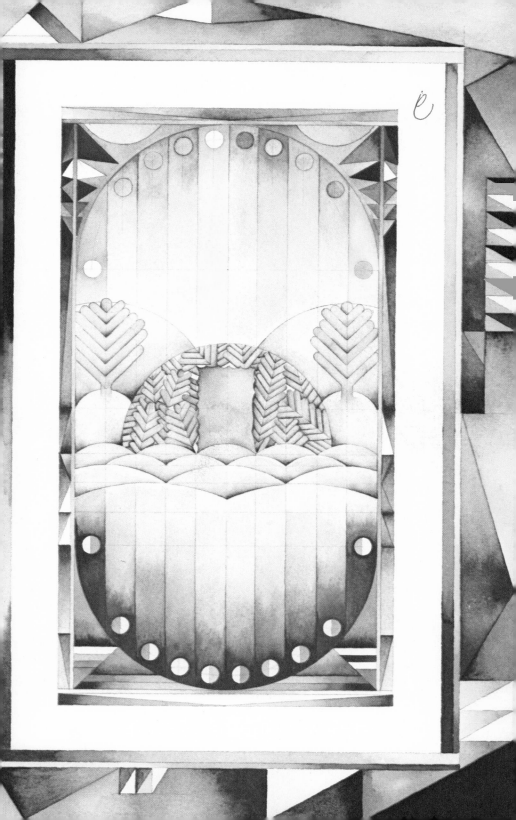

Ten nights for the clan spirit to choose! What would he dream of? A bird? An animal? A plant or a fish? Three times must the clan spirit appear . . . O–go–ne–sas planned what he would do.

"If the deer is chosen for me, I will wind myself in its soft skin to warn away the cold winds. If it is the bear, I will make a string of its strong claws to wear around my neck. If it is the wolf, his white teeth will guard me from danger. If it is the turtle, his shell could be my breastplate! Or maybe it will be a bird, and I can wear his wings . . . "

O–go–ne–sas' thoughts were full of nothing but hope and faith in his dreaming. But nine suns lighted the forests, nine nights darkened the lodge. The tenth day dawned frowning and gloomy, and the chiefs came.

They shook the lodge poles and called him to appear.

"Not today," he answered. "I have fasted and dreamed, yet the clan spirit came only once. Return tomorrow."

The next day they came again. "One day more," begged O–go–ne–sas. His voice was very low.

"Your time has passed!" the chiefs declared when they arrived the following day. But O–go–ne–sas pleaded with them.

"One day more. If the spirit has not come to me by then I will go—tomorrow I will leave with you."

His voice had grown even weaker, and the chiefs were worried. Must they release him? It was a disgrace to have no dream sign, no power he could call upon during his life! Could his clan spirit have refused to come to him? Cautiously, they parted the hemlock branches. O–go–ne–sas was painting his body—painting himself red as though he were dying!

A day later, the chiefs again shook the lodge poles, but this time there was no response except the trembling of hemlock branches. A strange silence seemed to have fallen in the forest. They entered the lodge. O–go–ne–sas was gone. As the chiefs stood there, silent and wondering, a bird flew down, and settling on a low branch began to speak to them:

"I am Jis–go–ga," it began. "I am he whom you seek."

"But we are looking for O–go–ne–sas," said the chiefs.

"I was O–go–ne–sas," the bird answered. "But my body is no more on earth."

"But why?" they asked him. "Why you, our best?"

"I fasted and waited," Jis–go–ga told them. "But my clan spirit came only once to show me my totem. I knew not the reason. I had done no evil and my spirit was pure. Then death came to rescue me from disgrace—for Jis–go–ga the Robin, who was to have been my totem, had hidden from the winter winds and no one could find him!''

''And now you are Jis–go–ga?''

''Yes. He has received me into his spirit. Now I am Jis–go–ga. I am the Robin.''

''You were brave,'' sorrowed a chief. ''We should have taken you sooner.''

''No, do not be sad,'' Jis–go–ga comforted him. ''Do not mourn me. When I return I will bring the Spring to you,'' he chanted. ''I will carry the gray shadows of Spring morning on my wings, and at the sound of their rustling, the snow on your path will melt into singing streams!

''I will not hide in the forest. I will nest by your lodges so your children will know me. They will know that Spring is coming when they hear my voice.

''I will sing to the trees, and new leaves will come forth to listen. I will swing on the wild cherry, and its blossoms will welcome me.

''And all will know me by the red glow on my breast, the color I painted my body be-cause I was willing to die.''

The chanting ceased. Jis–go–ga was gone. Clouds along the western sky nestled nearer the sun. In the silent forest, frozen streams melted suddenly, and the trees sent forth their young leaves. O–go–ne–sas' hemlock lodge fell to the earth, and even as the chiefs watched, all nature began its song of Spring.

ach sunset Gi–da–no–neh came to the lake to wander along the shore and listen to the song. Over the peaceful rhythm of the waves, the sweet song comforted her, for Gi–da–no–neh's life was not a happy one. Furs and rare feathers and a lodge had been promised her by the man her father had chosen to be her husband. But his feet were too slow for the hunt, his spirit too still for war. Old age was close to him. And his heart was dead.

Gi–da–no–neh delayed. She was young, and the world lay bright before her. Must she live in an old man's lodge? It was hard to disobey her father. Only the pleasant song of the water eased her troubled heart. It even seemed to grow stronger and more lively the longer she remained at the shore.

And so the days passed. One evening, returning from a long visit at the lake, she found two fish lying in the path. Never had she seen such beautiful fish! Their scales were shining silver brooches—rows of them—that seemed to have caught the sunset fire, so brilliantly did they glisten!

Gi–da–no–neh glanced around in alarm. Had someone been following her? No, all was still. Quickly she pulled the glistening brooches from the fish and attached them to her own frayed and faded doeskin dress.

What a wonderful find! Nearly bursting with joy, Gi–da–no–neh admired her glittering dress and then turned to look at the fish again. They looked good to eat and she was hungry, so she made a fire right where she was and had almost finished eating when her father found her.

He gazed in astonishment at the beautiful shining brooches. Who had thus adorned his daughter? Surely, some evil spirit was trying to tempt her, and would lure her away if he didn't stop it! In fear and rage, he ripped the brooches from her dress, threw them into the lake, and led his weeping daughter back to the lodge.

There, Gi–da–no–neh grieved and was not content. She mourned the loss of her brooches and begged her father to let her return and find them again. He refused. Day after day, she pleaded with him—she had to return to the lake, for now she felt drawn by some strange power she could not resist. And the fish she had eaten had carried such a thirst! She could no longer satisfy her craving at the little spring that trickled near the lodge. She tried to drink, but the water tasted so bitter!

At last Gi–da–no–neh grew desperate. One sunset, unable any longer to obey her father, she slipped away and ran as fast as she could to the lake. Gasping and stumbling, she fell down at the shore, buried her face in the water, and drank and drank as if she would never stop. Without even knowing it, she drifted into the lake and began to sink, when she felt strong arms thrown around her and heard someone speaking. Frightened, she tried to break free, but again the voice came, a beautiful musical voice. It was like a song, calling her: "Gi–da–no–neh, do not be afraid Gi–da–no–neh! It is I, Ga–ye–was the Fish! Do not be afraid of me—I love you!"

Amazed, Gi–da–no–neh stopped strug-

gling. Cautiously, she opened her eyes, and there was a tall young man, a brave as of her own people, but splendid with those same shining silver brooches covering him all over! Gi–da–no–neh gasped. Ga–ye–was, most mighty of all fish, ruler of the lake and the mountain streams! And he had said he loved her!

"Before, my life was so lonely," Ga–ye–was told Gi–da–no–neh, holding her gently in his strong arms, in the water. All my vast and beautiful possessions never satisfied me. I was never happy.

"And then you came. One day as I floated here singing my power song, I saw you standing over there on the shore listening to me. You looked very sad. I swam closer. You were so beautiful!

"From then on I waited here each sunset to sing for you. Then I left you the beautiful fish, for I knew that having once eaten them you would ever thirst for the lake water and never again be content with the land. For I had determined that you should be my bride!"

Gi–da–no–neh could not resist and agreed at once.

"Now you will again wear the brooches of which you were so cruelly deprived!" exclaimed Ga–ye–was. And at the sound of his voice many more shining brooches appeared everywhere on her dress, glistening and sparkling in the clear water. Suddenly Gi–da–no–neh found herself gliding with him down into the coolest depths of the lake. "You shall come with me to visit all the lands of my domain and will be my companion forever." So said Ga–ye–was, and Gi–da–no–neh was happy in her love for him.

The day was well up in the sky when Gi–da–no–neh's troubled father returned once more to the lake. He had wandered all night searching for his daughter. Suddenly he thought he heard her voice, but it seemed to come from the water. He gazed at the lake, and then stepped back in amazement as the waters parted and revealed Gi–da–no–neh, covered with silver brooches and glistening in her lover's arms!

"Father," she called to him. "It was not an evil spirit, but Ga–ye–was the Fish who lured me away. My true lover rules these pleasant waters, and I am now his bride. I will return no more to my land life, though I will always be near to help you. I could not go to the old man's lodge, Father. You loved me but you did not know my heart! Good-bye. Farewell!"

Slowly, as she finished speaking, the waters of the lake washed over the glittering brooches of Gi–da–no–neh and Ga–ye–was, and a gentle song was heard on shore over the peaceful rhythm of the waves.

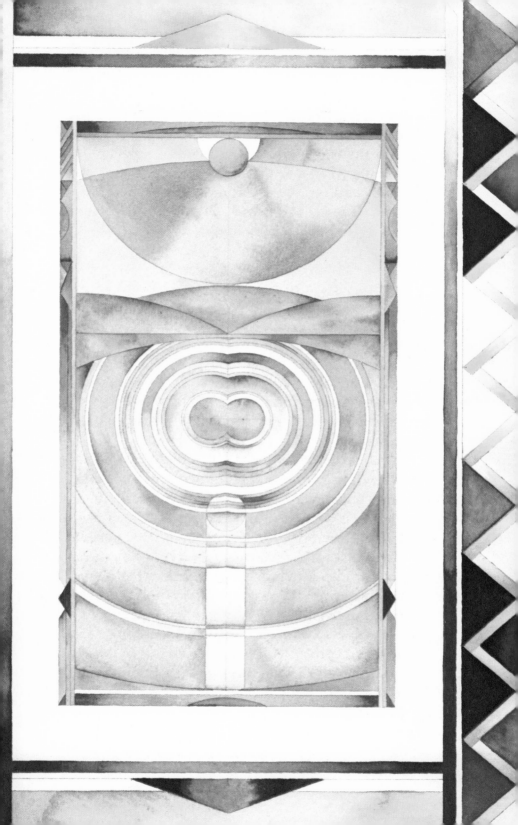

n the early days of the
earth, the Sky Holder di-
vided the forests. To each
clan he gave certain lands,
and the people lived in
order and peace. But
the Evil Minded, who
was jealous of the Sky
Holder, decided to put an end to this
harmony. He went to a few men in each
clan and told them that their share of
the forests was unjust, and that the other

clans had much better hunting grounds.

These evil suggestions caused suspicion, fighting, and bloodshed among the clans. Now in those days there were only small numbers of people, and when a man or woman was killed, it was a loss that the clan felt deeply. When the ground became red from many deaths, the people sorrowed.

The Sky Holder, seeing their trouble, then sought to restore peace. "Let us have a great dance," he said, "and in the pleasure of the ceremony, friendships will be renewed. Each clan must choose its best dancers for the competition. The winners' prize will be a broad strip of land and high mountains on each side of a great river filled with fish."

"Niuh, niuh! It is well, let it so be done!" The clans hailed the Sky Holder's suggestion. Their most agile braves prepared for the dance, and a feeling of good-willed rivalry came over the people.

First to enter the circle were the dancers of the Bear clan. The others competed, but none could equal the Bears until a group of braves who had banded together began their dance. It started with a slow, shuffling movement that gradually increased, and soon their twisting, bounding, leaping, sliding, gliding feet seemed scarcely to touch the ground. The people watching held their breath in astonishment. Never had they seen such dancing! Faster and faster moved the braves until in a wild delirious whirl they leaped into the air like demons, and as the last tap sounded upon the taut, wet head of the woodchuck-skin water drum, they brought their feet down in unison and finished the dance!

People yelled and shouted, and there were cries of, "Here are the winners!" "They have danced as men never have before!" "Give them the prize!" "They have won, they have won!"

Then the terrible thing happened. Filled with the spirit of the Evil Minded, the wild dancers sounded a signal with their rattles. Then they raised their clubs and struck down and beat to death a score of braves! They were even turning to slay others, but were halted by the Sky Holder.

"Cease!" he commanded, his voice angry and threatening. "Let the people come about me. You, evil ones," he thundered at the dancers, "come before me! Without cause you have made the ground red with the lives of your cousins and brothers, the most evil deed that men-beings have ever known. See how the people are grieving!

"We were gathered to strengthen our friendship and become one nation again. You chose a time of peace for a time to kill!"

The Sky Holder looked long at the dancers and then made his decision. "You have won the lands on each side of the river, but you shall not enjoy them as men."

The people wondered. Again the Sky Holder spoke:

"You are hereby outcast! You shall forevermore be stoned and trodden underfoot. But unlike others of your kind, you will give warning before you strike by shaking your rattles, even as you did when you murdered your relatives. You will be hunted and killed whenever you are seen, for everyone will know that you have the evil mind within.

"Depart now, outcasts! Take the lands you have won but go not as victors. Go as a wretched tribe upon whom war will ever be waged!"

One by one, the blood-guilty shuffled into line and began the devil song, ji–ha–yah. Chanting, they danced away into the shadows, out of sight of the sorrowing people. When they had reached a clearing, the Sky Holder shook the earth, and the evil dancers fell on their bellies. Their rattles dropped at their feet. Trembling, their faces in the dust, they felt the power of the Sky Holder. The very fibers of their bodies ripped, and they twisted in agony as their clothing grew fast to their skin and became scaly. Legs merged with the rattles where their feet had been, arms melted into their sides. Their tongues divided, their teeth fell out, sharp fangs pierced the bleeding gums, and now they were rattlesnakes, the Evil Minded's children, despised and hated crawlers of the ground!

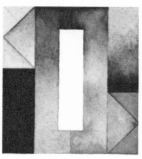n old times there was a young chief, a hunter of great cunning who killed many animals. But though he killed animals in order to eat, he never took advantage of them. He always asked their permission before hunting, made a ceremony, and threw tobacco. He never killed a swimming deer, or a doe with a fawn, or any animal tired out from a long run. After the hunt, he fed the

fish and water animals the inner parts he did not eat, and the flesh he could not use he left for the wolves and birds, calling to them: "Come, my friends, I have made a feast for you."

In the same way, when he took honey from a tree, he left some for the bears. After the corn harvest, he put open ears in the field for the crows so they wouldn't have to steal the young sprouts at the next planting. He threw tobacco for the animals of the woods and water and made incense for them with the o–yank–wa–o–weh, the sacred tobacco, and burned it even for the trees. As he was with animals, so he was with people. His tribe was loyal to him, for he remembered them and gave them meat. He was known widely as "Protector of the Birds and Beasts," and so he was called.

In those times, Ongwehoweh, the Iroquois, began to travel—sometimes to the southwest, where they learned things from other people, found new plants, and discovered different kinds of corn and beans. In these distant lands, they came across some friendly tribes and some unfriendly. One time the young chief was with an exploring party when a band of very angry people attacked them. He could not fight strongly because he was tired and very hungry from the long journey. The enemy separated him from his tribe and struck him down with a toma-hawk blow.

Now this enemy knew him because he had fought bravely at other times and had killed some of their people, so they were glad when they killed him and prized his scalp. They cut a circle around his scalp lock, tore it off, and held it up over a line of trees to prove to his braves that he had been killed. But his body lay in some thick bushes, and none of his tribe knew where it was.

Black night came. Alone the chief lay dead, his blood clotted upon the red and yellow leaves that covered the ground where he had died. Night birds scented the blood, the owl and the whippoorwill hovered over the body, and Sha–dah–ge–ah, the Dew Eagle, swooped down from the regions above the clouds. "He seems to be a friend," they decided. "Who could he have been?"

Not far away, a wolf sniffed the air and thought he smelled food. Creeping through the trees, he came upon the body, dead and scalped. His nose was upon the clotted blood, and he liked blood. Then he looked into the face of the Man. "Oh, no!" He leaped back with a long yelping howl. "Oh, no, my friend! The friend of the animals is dead here!"

His howling brought all the animals of the big woods—bear, deer, fox, beaver, and the big horned moose. The birds dropped

down around them. Sha–da–ge–ah had called crow and buzzard, the swift hawk, snipe, and the white heron. They held a council about their killed friend.

"He is our friend."

"He always fed us."

"We should not allow him to die."

"We ought to restore him."

These were some of their words. Then the wolf came up to the Man's body, and spoke gravely:

"Here is he who always gave us food when we were hungry, who was always thoughtful of us. We called him friend. Shall we be friendless? It is our duty to give him his life again."

So they all agreed: "He must not be lost to us. Let each one give his strongest medicine. We will bring him back to life."

Together the animals made a substance of great power though it fit into the bowl of an acorn. To prepare it, some gave their lives and were mixed with the medicine roots. When it was done, they carefully poured it down the throat of the Man. Bear, feeling over the body, found a warm spot over the heart. He took the young chief close in his hairy arms and hugged him so that the warmth might spread. Then owl remembered, "A living man must have a scalp."

Crow flew away for the scalp but could

not find it. The white heron went but while flying over a bean field she felt hungry and stopped to eat, and after having eaten found she was too heavy to fly again. Everyone grew impatient at this delay, so the pigeon hawk, swiftest of the birds, said that he would go and surely find it.

By this time, the enemy had become aware that the animals were holding a council over the chief. They were carefully guarding the scalp. It was stretched upon a hoop and swung on a thong over the smoke hole of a lodge. The pigeon hawk flew in wide circles until he discovered the drying scalp. Hovering only for a moment over the enemy's camp, he dropped down, snatched the prize, and shot upward into the clouds, faster than the arrows flying all around him. Without stopping to rest, he returned to where the other animals waited and dropped the scalp in their midst!

They tried it right away but it was so smoky and dried that it would not fit. They thought for a moment. Then Sha–da–ge–ah plucked a feather from his wing and dipped it in the pool of dew that rested in the hollow on his back. He sprinkled the water, and the dew came down in round drops, refreshing the dry scalp as it does a wilted flower. They tried it again but it kept slipping off, so a big crow emptied his stomach on it to make it stick fast. When they tried it once more, the

Man began to breathe faintly, and they knew that he was really going to live again.

The first thing the young chief felt when he woke up was a warm liquid trickling down the back of his throat. He heard the language of the birds and animals, but his eyes were shut, and he could not see them. Then he felt very warm, and there were friendly arms around him, but he did not know whose they were. After a time, a strong, hairy hand like that of the bear lifted him to his feet. But when he recovered his full life and opened his eyes, he found himself alone in the forest. Around him were many animal tracks, and a feather from Sha–da–ge–ah's wing lay at his feet.

ABOUT THE AUTHOR

Hettie Jones, born in Brooklyn, N.Y. and a graduate of Mary Washington College of the University of Virginia, began her career as an editor of a jazz magazine. She then became manager of *Partisan Review* and with her husband began a small publishing house. Ms. Jones has written several books for young people, including THE TREES STAND SHINING. A former teacher, she lives with her daughters, Kellie and Lisa, in New York City.

ABOUT THE ILLUSTRATOR

Nicholas Gaetano was born in Colorado Springs, Colorado and attended the Art Center College of Design in Los Angeles. He has been a free-lance advertising illustrator, traveled through Europe and South America and now makes his home in Oxford, New York.

LONGHOUSE WINTER is the first book he has illustrated with the hope of many more to come. His technique is geometric, very tightly controlled watercolor which incorporates some original designs used by the Iroquois in their crafts.

ABOUT THE BOOK

These tales, as adapted by Hettie Jones, were originally published in IROQUOIS' MYTHS AND LEGENDS, collected by Ya-ie-wa-noh (Harriet Maxwell Converse), an adopted Seneca of the Iroquois nation.

DE